The End Of Rude Handles

Jen Tynes

First Edition.

Red Morning Press is an independent publisher of contemporary poetry.
Its partners thank Roxanne Rash and McNaughton & Gunn Inc., Saline, Mich.
Cover Photos: Conan Kelly

Library of Congress Cataloging-in-Publication Data
Library of Congress Control Number: 2005937766
Tynes, Jen
The End Of Rude Handles / By Jen Tynes
p.cm
ISBN 0-9764439-1-0
I. Title

Red Morning Press
1140 Connecticut Ave., Suite 700, Washington, DC 20036
www.redmorningpress.com

Acknowledgements
Sections of this long poem have appeared or are forthcoming in *Verse Magazine*, *Jubilat*, and *H_NGM_N*. I looked to *Handicrafts of the Southern Highlands* by Allen H. Eaton for general divination and guidance and specifically for its first appendix, "Selected List of Names of Coverlets and Counterpanes Gathered From Many Sources." I am especially thankful for the eyes and ears of Conan Kelly, Erika Howsare, Monica Berlin and C.D. Wright.

“They who know of no purer sources of truth, who have traced up its stream no higher, stand, and wisely stand, by the Bible and the Constitution, and drink at it there with reverence and humanity; but they who behold where it comes trickling into this lake or that pool, gird up their loins once more, and continue their pilgrimage toward its fountainhead.”

-Henry David Thoreau, “On the Duty of Civil Disobedience”

CONTENTS

ALL MAY BE MERGED

Green leaves appear to nod and define.

When I snap pictures *tender* soars *apart at the roots,*
a small hand gathers a handhold.

Each other's bodies described
in the base languages of children, saying what

we make do with using well.

Fine white hairs on short green leaves.

When I speak of you some object is
also formed in light of that.

I enfold the brimming object to you.

I.

Between times

I took care
of small business: shining
blue eggs, fighting with a glass
jaw. Too pronounced

to holler at a full, heavy
house after midnight.
An elbow ratchets
my privates in their black cases.
The joint, if extended, means a body

tries a mouth.
Soon demand will cease
being a word
that brings me currency,
I will be cut
off and treated. Sashes

ceremoniously gather around
my steps and what am I
supposed to covet next?
Another slang for storm.

It comes in sheets
I picked *out of covers myself.*

Zion Rose Single

Chariot Wheel Ocean

Wave Acres of Diamonds

THE UNIVERSAL LOVE OF COLOR

Passing through
a screen of different trees,
sleeping on our sides.
The hot, red trigger

that plays someone else's music.
Instead of exhibition
: rubber belts. Iridescent shiners
climb the understatements of the body.
If the reader could not read

figures snapping across
the road : beneath tires : A friend
develops mammaries in order
to breathe. Also battering

pieces of meat and boxes out
further : in the yard : *and no other*
body has proceeded
as cautiously.

blue-pot

into *Maiden's Fancy*

Absolute quality is not alone

wooly

indigofera

jumping from the sheep's back

HOUSES ARE STILL STANDING

No one traveling
through the country
eats at the side of the road.
A blanket demeans
a body with small stains
that carry across the lawn.
It doesn't scream anything

in particular when I buy
condoms from the machine.
In a primitive way we knew

what was coming.
After our excursion
through the Alleghenies,
indelicate dreamlife
in which cancers

grind each other
in the wash.
Growing out of the practice
of gathering long
tables to my chest,
my gratitude

for the idea that attaches itself
to the animal is no longer
borne out

by any solid article.
I take your hand.

Little Blazing

Star Above Jethro

Collins of Hindman

Kentucky and Sam

Russell of Marion

An open box is a signal

of friendship—*Nameless Wonder Sixteen*

Chariot Wheels *Friendship*—Shot off to

drink and mend, *Bachelor's*

Buttons a woods full

of busted engines. *Whig Rose, Wide World's*

Wonder
In rare cases from the so-called window—

Catch Me If You Can

Huckleberry
All of it

moves us, but usually of

the same materials—*Rising*

Sun Rich Man's Fancy Wonder

Of The Forest.

To pass on

their dialect
Delegates shackle

the tongue.
"Tonight the light

is wildly bright and cavernous."
Body-like, a fish

that promises
it will keep on
breathing through

the long period
of transplantation.

"Extend, repeat."

Consider at its
quickest length.

Pushed a chair away from the table

Democratic

Victory

II.

IT IS NOW AMONG ADULTS

In a quart
of strawberries buried
some frogs.
Forty years round

a post in the bottoms
and then
corn split and then
rain. A stripped switch

eventually brings blood.
The back is carried
like the rest of the body,
wrought
from the floor.
Do you think this

is sound. Often
nesting them
I begin to feel
a crepuscular
machinery give
out.

Little pots
of fire.

Ten inches
across by six
inches deep.

Daniel Boone Church

Windows

Below Bristol *Taylor of Berea*

Kentucky W.C. Singleton

of Viper

TO FINISH THE DAMAGE

I saw you
head-off.

A beautiful contrast to white
eggs in parcels, *out-*
of-hand. The impulse

to interpret in this new medium.
I remove myself from anything
that rustles off the body
or table. Imitate
something:

argument-making, gathering bills.
Here's an example of my evening,
an extraordinary combination of delicacy
and strength—

I find the leaking spot
in the wall and the moldering fishing
pole. Nothing is prefaced
but hits at it again.

Creek or dimity
selves

nearest approach to Lathe or

"lay" a

Gentlemen's Fancy

ground bird

means weight

THE KEEN UNPASSIONED BEAUTY OF THE GREAT MACHINE

Propelled by hand
and eventually back

home to me. A figure
is a popular thrill.
The three of them

kept coming
to supper.
Kept eating

at me til gone: a follicle,
the shape
of my kin again.
Leaving

the natural horns
in foliage,
kissing

babies in
the face. The rosy
pucker when
I try.

Your ornery biddy
saves bones.

Eight Ways of Contrariness Lee's

Surrender Mary Lincoln Isle of Patmos
Charity Wheel Democratic Victory

Doors and Windows
Acres of Diamonds

Bonaparte's March Big Works
of Tennessee Liberty

Lilies of the Valley and of the Meadows Little
Girl's

Fancy Double Chariot Wheel
Pomegranate
Roses and Pinies in the Wilderness

Spiderweb

Snail Trail and Cat Track

Tennessee Trouble in North Carolina

Sunrise
on the Walls of Troy

Taste of
your supper,
lanterns

are like
that.
It is wrong

to send mixed
messages to the enemy,
houses
can change.
Vented barns

with people
inside. Chew
on good blades,
feast in dry

grass.
A deep light
collects beneath

the ceiling.
Bright leaf,

burley, fire.
A girl picking up

the leaves
machines miss,
first pass.

Young Lady's Perplexity—

Huckleberry

SOMEONE CALLED RADAR RADIATING FROM THE HIDE

Combination of an open
box across the cheek, right-handed
symptoms

include speed. My skin was not buried
before me but a legion
goes through the dirt. Firemen eating fish
dredged in flour
in the parking lot, I give thanks

you weren't sick with something
when you got to know me.
The extensive intercourse
grown up from a scarcity of cars,

the rigid pose of being on
television. I didn't always walk
this way, even monkeys in
their trees
understand what foreign

means. Not without
harm to their bodies.

"a deep turky red to a delicate pink"

some Madder

Dark splatter
or seep along
my pantleg is animal
in nature,

nature coming
home to eat.
These designs still drag

enough root to shame me,
and work is carried on
in connection.
Women as waterproof

as pails, men
as waterproof as water.
Figurine,

you smell the same body
breaking, occasionally
fresh when the animals
change.

Caught in the
act of emphasizing.

Job's Trouble Big

Works of Tennessee Snowball

and Pine

Tree border Sixteen

Chariot Wheels Sixteen

Snowballs

CONVERGING INTO THE GROUPS AND CENTERS

A bundle of hose left
twisted and loose to remind us,
periwinkle is a color
-dressed grass.
The neighboring children dress

like a faucet, with little things
in their hands and pockets.
We turn on every
light in the house
and leave them burning.

I take a bundle
of sticks and redden
their ankles if they misbehave,
I can only love
one person at a time.

Poppy

Petals Birch

Inner Bark

Alder
Sorrel
Madder

III.

AFTER DARK

a white thing on the line.
Whatever's toxic
in the canvas bellies up.
Even a herd of cattle

on borrowed land
knows dissension, makes eyes.
Electricity requires slicing back
the roundness of trees,
door to door and afterwards

a closet full of matchbooks,
strike at the very root
of your person.
There is no section
of the country where I do not sit

in a bucket bathing.
Days of creature comforts.
Your incandescence
is a body on the riverbed,

other sections
devolve and pass under.

WE ADOPTED

THE INSPIRING PRINCIPLE

For months

freon runs after dark,
clocking every gas station.
FOR TRADE SMALL DOGS
left on her pillow like a dream.

In the morning wetted everything
black to its stems.
Dried meats kept in dashes.
I am a harness

I use to keep myself
collected. Fresh bags
still marking where
we stopped and started
all over the yard.
Turning over several times

throughout the night like a motor
I sort the window from its dressings
and watch you
cut a delible swath.

OBJECTS LEFT ON
THE CARPORT TO DRY BLACKBERRY BUCKETS ONE PIECE BATHING SUITS CAT OF NINE TAILS CRACKED PINBALL MACHINE
MEAT HOOKS NORTH AMERICAN FIELD GUIDE TO BIRDS
OPEN CASKET THE WOOD OF WHICH HAS NOT BEEN ENTIRELY SEALED

THE RECOLLECTION OF AN OBJECT FORMED FROM IT

I watch a cat sleeping

on your chest then tossed
across the sunporch. Shooting of

a dog bred to taste for
dark chickens, our side

yard chill.
Where we came from grew

first out of being tightly
tied, and I am so hard

for the extended family.
Choose not to make their feet

out of the body's timber,
instead use wires

from the junk drawer, twist

ties from the morning
mail, the siren

in my automobile.

A PAIR OF PORRO
PRISM BINOCULARS A CROOKED JOG

TO THE BIRDS

THE EVENING

flaps the corners like a sham.
Face expands into
pieces you cannot use.

On their backs with mirrors.
Inside: twelve

including parents, basketing
into selves.
They run straight and do not
cling to anything.

Like counted eggs, balanced upright.
The careful balance of a story.
A graceful, elliptical

form is endangered and metallic,
warbles at the children—go to bed.
A shortened season

all hanging from the trees,
the flat wide sound
of air. Heavier material
in it but desiring.

A crumbling chin or lip
to jut out, worrying a field.

A JOG IN THE LIGHT

PATH AND THROUGH EACH BARREL

Double Bow

Knot

TO MAKE AND USE THE BORING MACHINE

To provide work
for the impoverished return
to my arms. Bricks

are both uprooted and paved.
My dead
beefsteaks lolling
against the fence, toeing-the-line
that took an afternoon
to settle.
To call a snake a garden

variety and duck
into these handicrafts
for the evening is a gash
in me, I cannot pronounce an end
to naming it.

Several hands
of mine are moving in
and out of the woods
they work, a flat, metallic
one-piece that rips a new
one. They are driven

together to stay
without themselves in
the maple and

the cherry, in walnut, hickory in
the dead heart
of a felted boxsprings, someone
must have made for themselves

a long fierce handle.

PRACTICES IN DAILY LIFE

DO NOT PRESENT THEMSELVES

IN THOSE OBJECTS HOUR

GLASS WILD ANIMALS THE

FRESH

LOOK OF SOMEONE
SHAVING THE BED

UNDER THE DIRECTION OF A TURNED OUT EYE

What is registered
—a Jug In Green.

I have seen neither—
your hide stretched
over a fence
to stop twitching
at night—nor out
in the open, testing

itself for fastness
under some smart-alecky
sun. In a car
garage, folded

and considering
how to pile
everything into a bitter heat
huddle, a brush
fire. Nor animals

coming out of
polished wood,
learned by the girls

in their mountain.
Nor materials reserved
for a bunch of dark
photographs, he fidgets

with neither anonymity.
Nor your hair.

IN A FIELD A *QUEEN*

OF ENGLAND

DEEP TURKEY RED

TO DELICATE PINK

A CONTINUATION OF THE FINE ELEMENTS

Several more animals
moving out on the lawn.
Anger is not enough

to continue wearing things
straight out of the ground in loops.
Sharp angles that light without

any reflection.
If everyone agreed

to be bored by the radio
tonight, deer would scatter

through the atmosphere.
Hot, white faults.

IV.

BOUGHS OF HANDS AND ARMS HANG ABOUT OUR SIDES

There is a spread
and persistence
of items,
pearled

animals in a pearled bed.
If I put on
something special
for you,

stop jogging
the baby long
enough to suss—
This side

of the mountain
is blocked
off from all
the ones it loved
across

the field—
when the morning
was still early.

In her Bedroom Factory at Elk Garden, Mineral

County: Cuckoo's

Nest, privet

leaves

SOMETHING RUDE

sharpened to a clear point.
A basket filling corn.

When I was new at this I *dressed*
materials as if they were fish
split between useful packages.

Driving the children back
after a visitation, red raw
onions sweated then the phone.
Lost to outside influence

a motor crumbles, pieces,
recovers. Quivers the hair-trigger
of every remediated thing.

ARTICLES MADE
FROM BARK AND SEEDS

GOUGES AND OTHER

IMPLEMENTS SUPPLEMENT
MY HANDS

AROUND DINNER'S NECK BUT NOT WITHOUT

A SENSE OF HISTORY

WHEN YOU CALL IT DOES IT

DROP ITS EYES

WHO HAS BEEN DEAF FROM BIRTH

I don't remember any
coming in this bed,
the dark and light

children next door
all wearing white
things down.
Also have no names,
the sounds

we make when hauling
our blank instances
home again.
Your wear the loss
in color, I tie a bone

to its own meat in the water,
gather liquor from the eye.
Some could not live

where willows do not
grow but burn that
out of your system.

You are missing,
it is my.

A continuous economic pressure is between my skin and yours,

switches its tail.

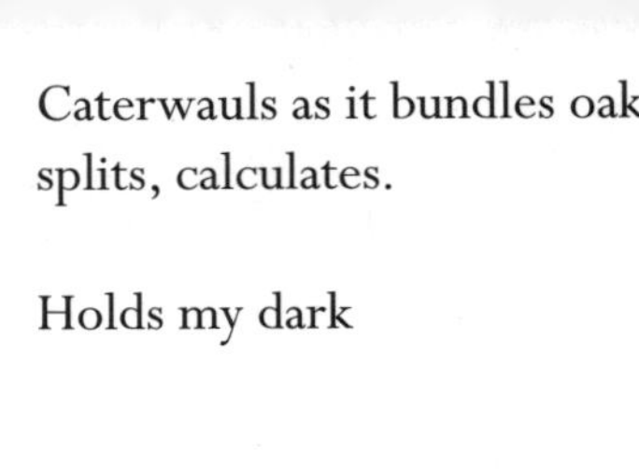

Caterwauls as it bundles oak
splits, calculates.

Holds my dark

bowl of an eye.
Valuable interpreters

lower their heads, cowlicks

shaved.

Cash needs are small-hipped and even
they divide

into censoriousness.

HANG DOWN YOUR HAIR.

WHEN STEPPING
INTO THE DOORWAY OF A HOUSE FULL

OF GIRLS ASK

WHICH IS THE MOTHER WHEN

DID YOU LEARN TO WARP ON A FRAME

THE END OF RUDE HANDLES

The dark spots the surface,
makes a lawn.

Some cousins used to trade
their prescriptions. Inside

the television is not encumbered
by any other boxes or rooms.

Your hands make
jars everywhere.

Floors, when they have risen
white, make white folds and charge

everyone that lit out
early. A party left thin, orange

stripes on the trees.
I burn my own

mark into each animal
long after thinking it.

Ways of Contrariness

To improvise is to pull out of thick air.

The problem with knowing your lines is knowing anything else. I grew up an hour's drive from the Museum of the American Quilter's Society, though I only visited once, on a school trip. I'd seen particularly nice quilts hung on walls before, but it was jarring to find them mounted in a hushed, white museum space, some kept under glass. The least conventional of the quilts were often the most vibrantly-colored, made not of outgrown clothes but fabric bought for the purpose of quilting it. The quilter in my family, my paternal grandmother, had eleven children reach adulthood during the 60's and 70's; she had to learn to work with polyester. She developed Alzheimer's early, and I can't identify the patterns she used. I hear that some families pass their patterns down by writing them in a code that outsiders can't decipher. Meaning: first item on the to-do list of any quilter's legacy: learn the code.

I don't write the way people talk; my intention is to make conversation, to make it over and over again until it *figures out*, fills out, shows itself. I don't talk the way I write or vice versa, but my spoken and written languages usually parallel and glare off each other. *Learn to work with polyester*. In both my writing and my speaking, lately, I've been trying to stay off-book a little more and make coherent eye contact. Everyone feels ambivalent about their lines. One summer long ago spent telemarketing and I still feel dangerous picking up a phone without a script in my hand. *What if someone sees it through?*

When I talk about conversation I mean the dynamics of exchange, what is taken away from us, how much give. The worst party guest, my spoken self has a tendency to either orate or—more likely—moon; before you know it the thrill is gone. Whereas on paper: *it tracks*, extends the possibilities. I found *Handicrafts of the Southern Highlands* on a used bookshelf, marked DISCARD, and for months I just looked at the pictures. Everything here has been worn out, has gotten so broken over backwards it thought it might die, *itself* included.

Conservation, Preservation, Reservation, Capitalization.
The importance of every little thing is always shifting. If you survive some depression or other and learn to make empathetic furniture out of privet wood and coffee cans, this knowledge must also be implicit within you: one day everyone will cut down their hedges for good or switch over to ficus; they will drink their coffee in beans and bricks. How you maneuver your *self-* and *knowledge*-at-large at this point says a lot about your method of imposition. I'm still new blood and I can't tell you what I'd do in your shoes, but I'm trying here to manage two things: always maintain a constant and a variable, make them both get up and walk around sometimes. Want to have a difficult conversation with someone, ask them what they mean when they say *traitor*.

All the italics are mine.
Would that every mirror were a two-way with some spilled sweat of ours on either side. I have been drawn into more than one conversation pitting introspective against extrospective seers, calibrating the resonances. Here, I'm thinking that one of a person's many interests is: not to form their allegiance, nor to make mirror and window interchangeable, but to place a mirror in front of a window and see infinity that way: a person's hand not only included but extended in its reach. For better or worse—when I get stuck I tend to look in the opposite direction.

There are several different ways of looking out a window.
Realize that no one ever steals our firewood. It isn't much of a burden to carry. It isn't worried over. It isn't marked. A cord is not akin to someone's favorite underwear flapping on the line; with wood we're talking about potential energy, true dispossession. My grandfather used to keep open fields full of half-tarped antiques that no one ever touched; one afternoon while he was Sunday driving someone cut the hearts from all his cows.

Myself, I think I'm neither savage nor ceremonial. I'm partial to stealing the heavy, charged parts of things that wouldn't walk off by themselves. The journals that farmers' wives used to keep in appointment books are often given away for nothing at junk stores and rummage sales because there is no blank space left to fill. I like to read how many inches it rained.

-

In a primitive way we knew what was coming.
Obviously, the more you extend the more you put yourself in contact. Sometimes I spend an evening out, but like a lot of people some nights I just stare at the two-way glass and think about cancers. What's the actual difference between a mountain and a molehill, how do I separate myself from it, using what kind of tools? Do I know the meaning of the ditty stuck in my head, and if a ditty how to fill it. How and what to say about simultaneity.

If you art it does it come back to you?
Incorporated fragments of commercially printed paper rule my afternoons, I reserve my mornings for *low relief, gluing wood* on top of previous wood for historical effect. The whole project *is scrapped* together with *staged fictional scenes* until I have a *real world* on my hands, which of course *implies that space will remain between some of the objects as part of the design.*

Or, another way to talk about collage: I'm constantly having a conversation with the person across the field.

Leave things out and watch the neighbors.
To the person across the field: Everything isn't sound after all; I'll just talk to you through this bone handle. I'll just jump right from the sheep's back. *I have made chairs from a pocketknife.* I have also used a pocket knife to make another blade's edge. If I borrowed someone else's material it's because it was right there *in front of me.*